DEATH OF THE KING

DEATH OF THE KING
AND OTHER POEMS

MIRIAM NEIGER-FLEISCHMANN

Translated from the Hebrew by
Anthony Rudolf and
Miriam Neiger-Fleischmann

Introduced by Lisa Russ Spaar

Shoestring Press

Printed by imprintdigital
Upton Pyne, Exeter
www.digital.imprint.co.uk

Typesetting and cover design by narrator
www.narrator.me.uk
info@narrator.me.uk
033 022 300 39

Published by Shoestring Press
19 Devonshire Avenue, Beeston, Nottingham, NG9 1BS
(0115) 925 1827
www.shoestringpress.co.uk

First published 2017

ISBN 978-1-910323-73-1

ACKNOWLEDGEMENTS

Thanks to the editors of journals where some of the poems first appeared:
Bitter Oleander; Modern Poetry in Translation; Stand; Winnicott Studies; Fire; New York Art Magazine; Jewish Quarterly; The Jerusalem Review; Ha'aretz; PN Review.

The poems were written over the last thirty years. The arrangement is not chronological. We worked on the poems sporadically but intensively. Miriam would send me a draft literal version with detailed comments and I would prepare a second draft. And so on, back and forth, by post then fax then email, until we were both satisfied. This book contains the poems which survived the process. Many did not. In the end, as it is in the beginning, poetry translation is "un travail d'écoute", as Pierre Leyris, distinguished translator of Donne and Eliot and Hopkins, once said.

– AR

To my grandchildren: Yair, Zohar, Avigail, Noam and Aviv

– M. N-F

CONTENTS

INTRODUCTION

Because I neither speak nor read Hebrew, I come to poet and painter Miriam Neiger-Fleischmann's work in much the same way that Neiger-Fleischmann – born into a family of Holocaust survivors in a border town divided between Hungary and Slovakia, and raised in Israel – experiences the world: in and through the warp and weft of exile, which is perforce a kind of "translation."

Even in these fine English versions – a collaboration between Neiger-Fleishmann and the British translator and poet Anthony Rudolf – the poems in *Death of the King* appear to transcend both their source and target language. It is a testament to the poet and her co-translator that these lyrical text(ile)s "read" like paintings, which of course require no single semantic flow.

Specifically, the poems feel drawn from the matrices of Neiger-Fleischmann's own visual grammar: canvases richly patterned, often evoking umbral, palimpsestic cityscapes seeping light, territories intensely bodily and deeply mysterious, places at once political and personal, thrillingly abstract and thrillingly physical. Whether overtly ekphrastic or not (the collection pays homage and refers to a myriad of painters and paintings), the poems in *Death of the King* possess a somatic materiality that is sown/sewn – that rends, mends, and bodies forth – from the page with a visceral psychological heft.

In a 2007 show, "Bordering on Embroidery," at the Jerusalem Artists' Gallery, Neiger-Fleishmann exhibited a series of paintings depicting spectral, splintered, oneiric heaps of buildings, in which the borders between inner and outer, domestic and exotic, body and landscape, word and world are often blurred and seem to suggest and unsettle each other everywhere. Materially, the pieces play frankly with notions of sewing and stitching, traditionally associated with feminine "decorative arts," even as they evince a daring female energy in the midst of landscapes charged with an ambiguous menace that feels gendered, environmental, and political.

A description of the show at the Jerusalem Artists' Gallery website tells me that the Hebrew word for embroidery is "rikma," which also denotes "tissue, in the anatomical sense. Thus its meaning is connected to the body, as in 'skin tissue.' It is also

1

connected to the 'body' of society, expressed metaphorically in 'the tissue [fabric] of life.'" I also learn that the studio where Neiger-Fleischmann created the work for this show is "near the virtual Green Line, in Beit Safafa, which was divided between Israel and Jordan from 1948 to 1967."

Neiger-Fleischmann's embroidery paintings signal a way of articulating the particular concerns and power of her poetry, which accrues its meaning in patterns of density and light, abstraction and image, hue and line. It is in this "tissue" of physical existence (the body, the object), sutured and threaded through by life's large abstractions – pain, vision, ambition, desire, ire – that the poems' force resides. 'My Signals', for instance, could be a linguistic embodiment of one of the "embroidery" paintings; it is Neiger-Fleishmann's mesh of physical detail (the snarling, reptilian airplane, emergency vehicles, the chock-a-block warehouses) and conceptual, large abstractions (desperation, fear, suppression, the cosmos) that effect in words the kind of primal, pre- or extra-literate response one has to visual art:

Summer night over Jerusalem:
In the sky a gloomy plane,
snarling like a lizard in the air,
a mutant dinosaur.
Emergency vehicles tear
the dark night apart with their howling
on a road illumined
to the point of desperation.
The warehouses of suppression are
chock-a-block: words
shower down
and scatter in a lake of memories.
Fear holds you
and stretches like the cosmos.
My body is sunk
in the fat flesh of night.
Decorating space, the stars
are sequins on an eastern veil.

It is hard to be comforted by their glow.
Their cold appearance will absorb my signals
after a hundred light years
and then it will be too late.

Jerusalem – City on the Hill, ancient site of holiness and strife – is a recurring motif in the collection. So is the plasticity of "dough" (another domestic association that Neiger-Fleischmann transforms into a larger creative force), frequent references to museums (galleries, houses, bodies) and the spaces and objects they contain, and the fairy tale, in which, again, traditional female myths are subverted and turned into potentially salvific sources.

Another key recurring trope in the collection is the sewn/sown star. In 'Warning', for instance, the poet evokes the yellow Star of David badges Jewish Europeans were compelled to wear to distinguish them from their fellow and sister citizens, conflating this historical image of oppression with a meditation on what can happen if words (like history) go unheeded:

This spring, the bushes
bend under the burden
of their own flowers,
bathe in the roses.

Veins of the desert wind
tint the sky
yellow. Helicopters
plough slowly through,
rend such thoughts
like a mourner's garment
at a Jewish funeral.

The words are weary, vague,
they shiver, sown onto
paper in tiny type.
Bright as the firmament,
Warnings shine and shimmer.

In her seminal book *Of Woman Born: Motherhood as Experience and Institution*, poet and activist Adrienne Rich writes, "Thinking is an active, fluid, expanding process; intellection, 'knowing,' are recapitulations of past processes. In arguing that we have by no means yet explored or understood our biological grounding, the miracle and paradox of the female body and its spiritual and political meanings, I am really asking whether women cannot begin, at last, to *think through the body*, to connect what has been so cruelly disorganized – our great mental capacities, hardly used; our highly developed tactile sense; our genius for close observation; our complicated, pain-enduring, multi-pleasured physicality." Through aesthetic gestures both interior and worldly (sewing and sowing), the poems gathered in *Death of the King* take up and extend Rich's call with a perspicacious somatic awareness that is as numinous and generative as consciousness itself.

– Lisa Russ Spaar, Charlottesville, Virginia 2016

EXILE

I am a poet exiled to fields of colour,
seed words in the furrow of the brush
sprout rhymed lines upon soft canvases
fertilise them with pigments,
make pictures grow.

I am a painter exiled from fields of colour.
I assemble words fallen from heaven
like rebel angels looking for salvation;
I arrange urgent letters on restless sheets,
build spectacles there.

I am a woman exiled from districts of love
to a land of rain colours, to sign-filled spaces.
I am doomed to collect in a charity box
scraps of spirit from reality's back rooms
to satisfy my soul.

*

One magical
morning in Ellul

I saw two pale
clouds kissing.

Deep ultramarine
was engraved

between them like
a river meandering

between two giant
mountains in a picture

taken from the air,
the blue narrowing

as they came closer
to each other

like the inspiration
of God's finger

in "the Creation"
in the Sistine Chapel.

In a moment of
grace they united:

one rain cloud
huge and black

MY SIGNALS

Summer night over Jerusalem:
In the sky a gloomy plane,
snarling like a lizard in the air,
a mutant dinosaur.
Emergency vehicles tear
the dark night apart with their howling
on a road illumined
to the point of desperation.
The warehouses of suppression are
chock-a-block: words
shower down
and scatter in a lake of memories.
Fear holds you
and stretches like the cosmos.
My body is sunk
in the fat flesh of night.
Decorating space, the stars
are sequins on an eastern veil.
It is hard to be comforted by their glow.
Their cold appearance will absorb my signals
after a hundred light years
and then it will be too late.

THE BENCH OF HOLMAN HUNT

I am sitting on the bench of Holman Hunt
in front of the Convent of Elijah.
Lifting up my eyes unto the hills,
I draw Herodion
and the outskirts of Bethlehem.
Herod's tomb is engraved
in the landscape.
Weeping Rachel, find me a place to live.
Miriam is in the barn,
holding a baby to her breast,
this time a Palestinian baby.
And the Magi are coming from the United Nations,
from the third world, Norway and America
and they adore
the olives and the history
and take a photograph, a souvenir
of a little Philistine, a boy
who has not yet learned how to throw stones.

DRIVING FROM TEL-AVIV TO JERUSALEM IN THE TWILIGHT

I am driven upwards
on a thin and ever narrowing thread
facing the hills. They wrinkle towards
the moon, to sacrifice a burden
and they strive hard as if desirous
of breaking through the limitations
placed on their rocky bodies.
The moon, full and round, is caught
on the windowpane. The red sun
is captured in the rear-view mirror,
sprung on the sky's slope
over a town yawning after a *hamsin* siesta.

In the space between sun and moon,
separated by shades,
creation is renewed.
Light clouds with their soft transparent colours
glide and let the heavy
darkness drop, slowly
flattening on the face of the road.
The border line between
light and dark is rising to the heavens
People are seen but do not see.
Are seen and do not see.
Do not see.

MEXICO JERUSALEM

I saw the sun sliding
behind the gray mountain.
I became the eyes
of a vanished Aztec
and through his eyes
the sun slipped away
leaving pale pink marks
on the place it abandoned,
pressure on my throat
and distress moving
towards the horizon
of the sun in the thick
of the mountain. And I saw
the arms of the Aztec
raised up in the bloody
paintings on the jars
and I heard the bells
of hell in the pyramids
and the weeping hearts
ripped out of bodies.
I trembled in the terrible
euphoria of power,
the ecstasy of guilt,
the pleasure
of giving pleasure
in the shrine of Tenochtitlan
facing cruel idols.
The spirits of nature
turned into matter.
Satiate them with corpses
and the sun will shine
and the rain
will be in season.
And I wondered at their vanity

in believing they will
raise the sun
and bring down rain
by means of sacrifice.
Here in Jerusalem,
"rain is falling
on the face of my buddies".

IN THE ANTHROPOLOGY MUSEUM

Proper objects are standing here, at a distance from their destination.
A collection blended together in a mythic dough ready for digestion.
Horrible rituals are pressed through the sleeves of the construction
into a compact, subtle, prophetic capsule of memory.
Curves of the legendary feathered snake cause confusion
around containers no longer in context,
proofs in the sentences of culture.
Tense beauty radiates from the rulers of the Kingdom of Entropy.
Hearts torn out are still quivering in stone basins,
offerings for the gods who keep the sunrise bloody.
Jade mosaic on a skull. The recycled dead
are revealed in the dust, serving in a latter-day cult.
Its worshippers are retired American women
admiring with such precise tone: oh, how nice!
Guided tour, a few steps forward, attracted
by the promise of a charm in the epic
of Montezuma's daughter, now curator.
And with each additional ride
following the objects of a ruined temple,
another unit of time is created in the beyond.
And what is ahead of us
becomes clear like the light flickering among the clouds
on a day which promises nothing in the way of good news.

IN THE MUSEUM

Inside the glass cases
in the temple of objects
the dreams of artists
of the past that came true
are captured.
Like doggies
in quarantine, they look
into our eyes and ask
silently: take us away.

VISIT TO THE FRICK COLLECTION
(NEW YORK)

"The Polish Rider" travels through infinity.
Spatial light around him, landscapes pressing on him,
Rembrandt observes him out of the corner of his eye
as present as a father keeping watch.
The Polish Rider will be the one who releases us,
unmoving rider on a chestnut horse, a noble creature.
He will be the one who releases me
to enter a place where all that's possible comes true.
In this palace on Fifth Avenue
all the dead masters are gathered
for an endless celebration of the soul
and the victory of visual memory.

GIVE ME THE KEY WORD

The Polish Rider keeps the password secret,
looks towards his adorers with eternal mildness.
Your loves, rider, have survived on the canvas
for more than three hundred years.
My loves are gone.
You'll gaze over me,
over the walls and the pain of other artists
to the big garden, the fallen leaves,
the trees raising bare arms
in a plea to heaven.
Please, let this winter come to an end,
let the emptiness – left in the quiver of Eros,
after he sent his arrows everywhere on earth and in the heavens,
waiting for their return loaded with love – come to an end.
Meanwhile he bites his nails afraid
that none of the arrows will be coming back.
Polish Rider, your quiver is full.

LIGHT OF THE LILIES

The water lilies have been anointed with yellow.
Red dots are flowers.
The water: blue and violet brush strokes;
and different kinds of green.
Your painted lilies, Monet, are flowers of evil.
Between the spots of colour
the unknown tiptoes
up to me,
allows the imps of Bosch
to complain before my eyes,
to tickle my restraint,
and when they leave,
their double meaning giggles through the air
like the Cheshire Cat in times gone by.
I weave among
the touches of colour
and turn,
a leaf of light
upon the water.

REMOTE CONTROL

for Motti

A creature saturated with its own significance
was entrapped like a bird in an airplane engine, no escape.
Inside an instrument for spreading images,
it flapped its invisible wings on the screen from within.
Passion and its substitute wriggled in its imagined belly
like the snakes around Laocoön and his miserable sons.
And when this creature started quivering and slowly dying
silently, in the soft darkness on my bed,
misled by lazy sparkles
and the tail of a marvel,
I sealed its fate.
I pressed the remote and in the twinkling of an eye
rescued an illusion from distress
sending it directly into space.

IN THE STREET OF LOST HOPE

In the street of lost hope,
at the palace of an Austro-Hungarian prince,
time and happiness
dance a waltz.
Step step time, step happiness: turn;
Step step happiness, step time: turn.
They are handsome, elegant and suitable:
lofty heroes, beyond reach, advance guard.
The soul is full of them.
Helplessness, by contrast,
faces them like a wall-flower,
and the place marks time.

BROKEN BIOGRAPHY

A woman undisciplined rebuilt
her house from crumbs of memory
bound with sentimental dough.

The memories broken into light
created a rainbow.
People were amazed that such a light
with its many hues could flow
from splinters arranged as a house.

*

A choir of dogs
barking in unison
opened the season

In a region
of smoky landscapes
I wanted to be with you.

While I am here
I hallucinate
landscapes.

Your shape is crystallized
for real by the waves
at the front of my brain.

A blue flame sprouting
from your fingers warmed
the potatoes

I was keeping
for cold winter nights
and the thoughts

poured out of my notebook
like volcanic lava
from a solid black highway.

INNOCENCE

I wasn't the queen of the class.
Always, little victories no one else
wanted were left for me.
I don't even remember myself as innocent,
not in the sense of being a girl,
not in any sense.
Or feeling clarity where there was fog.
I only knew fog,
that there were powers winding towards me
which in a second would cover me all over
like a drifting desert cloud.
When it was over I hadn't changed at all,
except for grains of dust and soot in every fissure of my body.
And between thin delicate leaves and the ruin of the façade,
in the shadows I possessed
the liberty of a delectable bubble
of soap.

BELONG

I am eating yoghurt with great longing,
pouring the white stuff into my guts;
they said there'll be a storm tomorrow;
the snow will cover my spaces.
White thought is waking up inside me,
ruling my moments, craving
that what you see is what you get.
If I can make this public,
keep in line with the surface of the landscape,
belong to its colours,
I shall at last
integrate my life, and relax.

GERMAN NATURE

German land generated within me a permeable tranquillity like the clover grass with its heart-shaped leaves, which penetrate with cosmic patience my organic hollows, plug roots between veins and tissues, and rise budding from my body. I was Little Red Riding Hood in a wood of deer and hares, leading a hound along tight paths. I was the burning blossom of the grass, snuggling up to the velvet moss over the tree stumps

My legs sink in dust
In my sack, ashes

SECOND GENERATION ARTIST

In the same language they admire my art
My dear ones fated to be murdered
Thoughts drill holes in my body
to store gun powder.

EATING

While keeping the tension in his body, not collapsing into slices,
he says: "I eat
like a steam train fireman who shovels coal
into the crater of the boiler.
I convey my family tree in railway carriages.
I arrange complex carbohydrates on trays, how tasty,
and stoke decorated proteins,
release the vitality of the cells on invisible tracks extending
to the horizon floating in the mist of years:
chew, chew, chew".

*

My pity is fake,
my poems atonement.
Mutation in my genes
began in the gas chambers.
Even before that,
antigens were
created in my blood
against torture and murder
and mindless oppression
and all kinds of atrocities.
Yet, nobody cares
if we count their dead
or our own dead.
See the dead
arranged in a row,
arranged in a pile
or burned in a pile.
Everyone wants
to keep evil at bay.
Therefore, I don't cry
over the Palestinians,
nor do I cry
over anyone else!
Because, if I cry
over my dead,
they will stand before me
in a long line
their fleshless corpses,
eaten by time,
as in a roll call
or on the "day
of visitation",

and their mute
muselmann hands
will offer
faded shreds
from an old shroud
to wipe my tears if I weep
If I weep

HOW CAN I…

How can I dip into
Les Fleurs du mal
or paint touches of sunset
in water colour,
while grandmother,
wearing her yellow star,
keeps a solemn eye on me
from beyond the mysterious
red horizon?
And even if, at one with her,
I were to weep,
could I freeze her moment
of insight when they took her
to "arbeit macht frei"
that there was no going back?
Her gaze
hovers over me
like a lighthouse
shooting beacons
into the darkness,
and dictates where I go.
Punctured
by genetic codes
that turn hazy
as the Blue Danube meanders,
I am compelled
to keep my memory
on full alert, to reconstruct
unceasingly
all that happened,
and take revenge
through creative existence.

NOT A LEGEND

While the earth of Europe was fertilised with ashes and dust,
the souls whose mission was interrupted
when they were still suffering separation anxiety
insisted they must find a new vessel
for permanent dwelling – a survival order, directed from on high!
When my mother was pregnant,
at least three of them were already sticking to her
in the valley of the shadow of death.
Inspired by hope for the future, standing at the entrance to her body,
each of them pushed past the ministering angel,
and protested about the wasting of good time,
with no other solution available and a shortage of embryos,
in haste, with inexplicable unanimity,
in the twinkling of an eye, going with the stream of
                                    consciousness, they trickled
together, becoming a tiny embryo, daughter of Phoenix,
who was destined to be raised up from the dust.
A poet, a painter and a scholar exposed themselves in my spirit
and perhaps in disguise to keep their names secret.
They crowded together and argued between themselves
for more than sixty years. Rarely will they come to consciousness.
When the fingers of one are starving for a paint brush
the other comes along, important, his throat filled with words.
Then the scholar calls out no! because the past invites you back,
struggling in vain with the needs of the body
which dictates its obligations
in feminine words with the female suffix,
motherhood, love.
That's the way I was born.

ROUTE

From the train window, on a parallel track
a dry bush that survived the summer, is rolling gently,
driven by soft, autumnal wind.
The bush stays on track, it is not
blowing in the wind, its seeds stay put
between the railway sleepers, to sprout in spring time.
But alas for the bush and its safe journey!
Here, everything that raises its head to grow
will be chopped off in the gallop of the wagons.
Oh, the fertility of travels and trials, routes and trails.

JOURNEY

In the airport, two planes on the ground,
craving to take off, spread their wings
to each other. The transparent
rainbow fades over a mountain of garbage.
Black clouds hurry to the mountains, to Jerusalem,
to unload a burden of showers;
at the same time they echo
the silent voice of earth and rocks.
Gloomy cypresses stab the mist.
Nearby the strap of road is loosened,
plods along the slope towards its end.
In the central station, a sign:
"Short-term Parking".

*

Belted shrunken
I sat inside
a shining fleecy cloud
steering over
white islands.

Down below
you assembled
broken marble columns
for building
steps to Olympus
as quickly as possible

to reach the oracle
at heaven's gate still

make the oracle tell
the Truth.

MEETING

Is the edge of an iceberg
colliding with an iceberg? Is the top
of a volcano bumping into
the top of a volcano, and in the crater
is the flame swirling around?
Or something
is emerging from the fog,
trying to make contact,
trying to send a signal
to a peak exposed in front;
bodies are swallowed in the chaos,
or perhaps a bud sprouts from the earth
near a bud of a different species,
or even the same, it's hard to guess.
The soil covers roots and tubers:
we do not know what is in their hearts,
what is kept and what rejected.
But, as a matter of fact,
they feel only the gravity of themselves.

HAMMOCK

You are the hammock where I lay my yearnings
during siesta on a summer's day
so that they shall have an airy shaking
in the midst of imaginary trees
in a surprise forest, supposing it is there

*

A cautious mermaid was thrown out of her realm onto dry land after a night of drunken revels. She hit the rock in a spiral movement and immediately vomited up the magical foreign words wriggling around inside her body. She raised her shoulders, took a deep breath and prayed to the great father.

Jellyfish and sympathetic crabs gazed upon her with pity when she tried, in a sudden caprice, to tear her virginity's coat of mail from her body.

ALICE

It's ten already. Alice is
a good girl neat and tidy, doesn't masturbate.
At this moment, she does not even have
fantasies.
   Now she is ready
to listen to a surreal story.
She has a watch, a telephone, a camera
and a computer,
     but her real contacts
she creates slowly, telepathically.
She ties pink ribbons on the legs
of pigeons at her window,
plugs the ears of little dogs with wool.
Her sun laughs only on Shabbat
and on weekdays is indifferent.
Her real friend is the moon
and the fact men landed on it
makes no impression.
Whenever she wants,
she walks on it herself,
peeps down from there on couples making love.
By now she has seen
all the positions,
taken part in real pleasures,
produced fake orgasms.
Sometimes she comes.
But what makes her really wet
are stories about wonderland
and the huge cock of a pervert
who desires little girls.

EVEN IN A FAIRY TALE

In a miraculous forest
under a blue sky
I collected purple longings in a bag
like mulberries or raspberries
in a book of northern fairy tales;
later I'll deliver them
to your safe keeping.

But the wolf got there first
and now
by grace of his teeth
I am studying
psychoanalysis
and I realize
why responding to the forest
is forbidden
to mature girls
dripping juicy colours
even in the closed area
of a fairy tale

GREEN MEMORY

I peel avocado pears
and cut them
into blocks, into squares.
Their greeny smell
is a warm winter,
a glance, a meal.
Ripe winter
emerged from the cycle,
survived its season
when we were lovers.
Each act is a poetry
lacking all pity.

FAR AWAY

1)

Standing far away
you can only see the bright side
as from a satellite one sees
the traces of the brush stroke of the universe
in the frozen streams of the North Pole
or the perfect shape
of whirlpools of dust
which cover the whole of China –
the rustle of angels' wings cannot
sweep it all away

2)

The sorrow was growing inside her
like vapour rises from dry land
which never reaches out and merges
with a piece of the celestial universe, and she knows
that in the nature of her desire
there is already a flaw,
just as separation is the essence of creation.
Better this way than Chaos.

RAPTURE

A doll whose revels now are ended
is taken from the shop window of my life
and carried under the arm of the assistant
– her joints stripped out, her backbone gone –
to the props warehouse.
There she'll babble mechanically,
performing a symphony of delusion
while wiping her halo with her hand
as you wipe away the cold sweat
which has stricken you
with the burn of your awareness.

CONCEPT

It feels good
to think of you
as a concept
beyond my reach.

Your physical presence
is hidden
in a projected image.

From now on, I'll love you
only in my secret zone,
only in molecules
with their grains of divinity,

in circular
units of light,
in the pain of your absence.

SHADOW CABINET

The time for the renewal of love
is the hour when shadows sharpen.
From the shade, silhouettes are rising,
their work done in desperate darkness.
They evaporate vanity, radiate flesh,
have the power to prevent destruction
and turn the ocean between us
into a salt marsh.
But when light comes,
their gaze is agonized and they draw back,
leave the memory of you
like a skipping game
with the poisonous snakes of the past,
that still run wild
and protect the vial of oblivion.

ORDER

For the love of a man I am like a chimney
destroyed by its own smoke
spiralling to nothing from the fire.
If I had a time machine
I would arrange the events
in a different order:
a little bit from the end in the middle,
a little bit from the beginning in the end,
balanced portions
from the hand of a gourmet chef
and in the chapters of the romance
I would divide in equal parts
the aroma of the agony of love.

THE POWER OF POETRY

What is the power of a poem
in the unordered spaces
torn between
tinted treetops and the sky?

What is the secret power
of shapes
constructed with black touches
on a Chinese scroll?

Shall solitude
do our painting for us?
And what is the essence of birth: pain
or new creation?

*

Avigail is painting stars,
big stars, in many colours,
posing on the paper
all over the place.
Avigail paints one star
in the centre, golden yellow,
radiant, and draws
a face on the star.
It is too soon
to warn her about black holes,
I guess.

THE MIRACLE OF A NEW-BORN SMILE

for Yair

A.

Light and rapid sparkles crossing back
and forth between our faces stitched the air,
eye to eye, brain to brain.
In the short distance between my large face, drawn with the
                                        dust of years
and your face, tiny and soft,
a point of understanding became clear.
Then your lips stretched towards me,
the moment when a touch of recognition
extended a few seconds.
You knew how to move, how to make the connection.
Another miracle has happened since you were born:
a smile.

B.

The image in the pupil
of the eye begins to sharpen.
The self's expansion wears a face,
treasures the experience of another body,
and DNA notes
will be played on your body.
All in good time, words fitly spoken,
and the words shaped in the gentle space of your mouth
will roll the muscles between your tongue and lips,
infiltrate the world of expression.

C.

Your smile will shine in a world
arranged in longitudes and latitudes,
a world with its powerful routines, passionately determined
to turn you into a cog, inserted into a slot,
shrunk to its shape.
But you will grow up beyond conformity
and corrode the very ground
to which you were pushed.
And the machine will never overcoming your increasing energy
and its iron power will be shaped by your thoughts,
rounded by your angelic smile.

MY GRANDDAUGHTER IS PAINTING
MY PORTRAIT

The generations gather in the room,
a family picture.
Zohar, beloved child,
is drawing in secret my portrait on paper
while my gaze drifts far away
to the TV screen aflicker
with other ways of being.
In the fullness of her nine years,
she looks at me, studies my outline
with creative passion,
studies the lines on my face
collected over decades,
and does not forget to emphasise
the wrinkles on my neck
and the darkness under my eyes.
This beloved child, staring straight at me,
draws and does not know
my portrait is already drawn within her.

TO MY SON OVER THE SEAS

For Lior

We walk only in the ways open to us.
The gaps between our steps
are stretched like stones in a sling.
The steps engender descendants:
cross-roads and distances.
Fata Morgana might help,
reflection of light from another continent,
a hologram of flesh and blood.
A gentle attempt needs to be made
to bring continents close
until they get used to the ocean.

MY AUNT'S HOUSE

My aunt and uncle were childless and silent,
always nodding to each other.
The walls of their house were infertile, painted like tapestry,
designed by the flicker of their eyes.
Their memories sat on the table in the living room,
gazing at them like everlasting candles
whose smoke turned what they saw into a day dream.
They did not scream, they had no reason to grumble,
they gave themselves permission to live from one day till the last –
when my uncle moved to the graveyard,
she continued to sit there. She remained silent for him.
And the walls dripped bugs
which fell on her bosom.
And the walls shrank
and pushed her to the old people's home.
A young couple is now living in the house of my aunt
and the walls are pregnant.

OBJECTS

The objects in my aunt's house died when she was alive,
since objects come to life with a touch.
For years they were corpses,
while she moved between sofa and couch,
looking at blurred grains
of dust in the air, and the cocoons
of the cockroaches remained after they were sprayed.
When she left for the old people's home
we rescued the objects from their barren existence
and moved them to a rubbish heap for company,
piled high like our guilt feelings for this action,
as heavy as the weight we ascribe to objects
even though they are not our subject of desire.
Now my aunt sits on her bed or in the dining room
with no objective.

DEATH OF THE KING

The glamour of his medals
casts gloom on Arab princes

All the days of the king
lie in velvet, on parade.

Phantom riders on noble
white horses float over

phrases from the Koran:
we belong to Allah

and to Allah we return.
The sound of a volley

of shots. In the mouth of
the grave, 'El Malik', the gate

of Eden, comes the Order
of *Kaffias* to bend the knee.

A whim of fate has inter-
mingled world leaders, bare heads

and covered, heads of nations:
spots on the screen, running

to and fro, like sperm destined
to be wasted, semen of

giants, seeds of royalty,
an oriental harem

of the most powerful men,
screens veil women inside

their palaces, they whisper
in elemental voices:

oh, what a concentration
of resources. Shepherd girls,

come quickly to the well,
hurry now, kneel at the mouth

of the well, pump their semen.
And then they lick their lips.

LAST HUG

There are moments in life
when the sediment of sadness
inside your body
competes with the blood
which is coursing through your veins,
arrives at heart and brain,
floods the organs and rises up from you
to the vast being of sorrow
sitting like a huge balloon between you
and the planets,
                   and arrests their movements.
Our private pain increases, becomes a tool,
bursting out of the body
as sharp as a scalpel piercing heaven's womb.
In return the wound
drips its own rain on us,
soaks us through,
as when a warm hug bears away
memories of the departures
of all the people you know you
will never see again.

WARNING

This spring, the bushes
bend under the burden
of their own flowers,
bathe in the roses.

Veins of the desert wind
tint the sky
yellow. Helicopters
plough slowly through,
rend such thoughts
like a mourner's garment
at a Jewish funeral.

The words are weary, vague,
they shiver, sown onto
paper in tiny type.
Bright as the firmament,
warnings shine and shimmer.

NOTES

Page 8, 'One magical/morning...'
Ellul is the last month of the year in the lunar calendar used in traditional Judaism.

Pages 12–13, 'Mexico Jerusalem':
the last two lines are from a famous poem by Yehuda Amichai, 'Rain on the Battlefield'.

Page 28, 'My pity is fake...':
"And what will ye do in the day of visitation, and in the desolation which will come from far": Isaiah 10.3 (King James version). "Desolation" translates the Hebrew word shoah, which has become another name for the Holocaust. Muselmann, was a slang word in Auschwitz and other camps for those skeletal figures who had given up in mind and body and would soon die or be "selected" for the gas chambers.

Page 30, 'How can I...'
'Arbeit Macht Frei': "Work sets you free": the cynical motto above the entrance to Auschwitz and other camps.

Page 31, 'Not a Legend':
line 8: see psalm 23 verse 4: "Yea, though I walk through the valley of the shadow of death, I will fear no evil, for Thou art with me; Thy rod and Thy staff, they comfort me".

Page 48, 'The Miracle of a New-Born Smile':
section B line 7: see Proverbs 25 verse 11: "A word fitly spoken is like apples of gold in settings of silver".

ABOUT THE AUTHORS

Miriam Neiger-Fleischmann

Miriam Neiger-Fleischmann was born in Slovakia, 1948. Her parents were Holocaust survivors from Hungary. She came to Israel in 1949, and lives and works in Jerusalem. She studied art at the Bezalel Academy in Jerusalem from 1977-1981. In 2015 she received a PhD at the Hebrew University of Jerusalem on the poetry of Avigdor Hameiri.

She has published three volumes of poems in Hebrew: *Words in a Visual Space*, *Images Reproduced* and *Material in No Man's Land*. She has won several prizes. One volume in Hungarian translation has appeared in Budapest, *Száműzetés* (Exile). For many years she and Anthony Rudolf have translated her poems into English, latterly exchanging emails containing revisions.

Pursuing a parallel artistic life as a painter, Miriam Neiger-Fleischmann has participated in many exhibitions at home – including the Israel Museum and the Tel-Aviv Museum – and abroad in New York, Paris, Germany, Spain, Hungary and Slovakia. Her work can be found in the permanent collections of the Israel Museum and the National Museum of Women in the Arts, Washington DC. Her website is www.miriamneiger.com.

Lisa Russ Spaar

Lisa Russ Spaar is the author of many collections of poetry, including *Glass Town* (Red Hen Press, 1999), *Blue Venus* (Persea, 2004), *Satin Cash* (Persea, 2008), *Vanitas, Rough* (Persea, 2012), and the forthcoming *Orexia* (Persea, 2017). She is the editor of *Monticello in Mind: Fifty Contemporary Poems on Jefferson*, *Acquainted with the Night: Insomnia Poems*, and *All that Mighty Heart: London Poems*. A collection of her essays, *The Hide-and-Seek Muse: Annotations of Contemporary Poetry*, was published by Drunken Boat Media in 2013.

Her awards include a Guggenheim Fellowship, a Rona Jaffe Award, the Carole Weinstein Poetry Prize, an All University Teaching Award, and the 2013-2014 Faculty Award of the

Jefferson Scholars Foundation. Her poems have appeared in the *Best American Poetry* series, *Poetry, Boston Review, Blackbird, IMAGE, Paris Review, Ploughshares, Slate, Shenandoah, The Kenyon Review, Virginia Quarterly Review*, and many other journals and quarterlies.

Lisa Russ Spaar's commentaries and columns about poetry appear regularly or are forthcoming in the *Chronicle of Higher Education*, the *Washington Post*, the *New York Times*, the *Los Angeles Review of Books*. She was short-listed for the 2015 National Book Critics Circle Award for Excellence in Reviewing, and has taught at the Palm Beach Poetry Festival, Seattle Pacific University, and the Vermont Studio Center. She is Professor of English and Creative Writing at the University of Virginia.

Anthony Rudolf

Born in London in 1942, Anthony Rudolf is the author of several memoirs, including *The Arithmetic of Memory* and *Silent Conversations: A Reader's Life* (Seagull Books/University of Chicago Press). He wrote the first extended study in English of Primo Levi. As a literary essayist, Rudolf has ranged widely: from Balzac and Byron to F.T. Prince and Borges.

His book of prose fables, *The Mermaid from the Azores*, awaits publication. He has written on visual artists, including R.B. Kitaj (National Gallery, 2001). He has translated several books of poetry from French and Russian, including selections of Yves Bonnefoy, Edmond Jabès, Claude Vigée and Yevgeny Vinokourov. He has edited various anthologies.

Rudolf's reviews, articles, poems, translations, obituaries and interviews with writers have appeared in numerous journals. In 1969, he founded the now dormant Menard Press. He is also the author of *Zigzag:* five prose/verse sequences (Carcanet) and *Jerzyk*, an annotated edition of Holocaust diaries (Shearsman Books). His *Collected Poems* will be published by Carcanet in 2017.